MW00882516

THE PENETRATING POWER OF THE WORD OF GOD

Unlocking The Secrets of using The Limitless
Power of The Word to Change Your Life Forever!

APOSTLE MARVIN L. SMITH

XULON ELITE

Xulon Press Elite
2301 Lucien Way #415
Maitland, FL 32751
407.339.4217
www.xulonpress.com

Paperback ISBN-13: 978-1-6628-7190-0
Ebook ISBN-13: 978-1-6628-7191-7

Table of Contents

Acknowledgments

Firstly, I want to thank my Lord and Savior, Jesus Christ. Thank you for giving me the unction to write this book, that it may be a blessing to Kingdom citizens.

I would like to acknowledge my beautiful wife, Denise Smith, for her support and patience during the writing of this book, I also want to thank my children, grandchildren, sisters, and brothers for their outpouring of love and support.

Special thanks to Bishop Carl and Barbara Vann who were instrumental in establishing a foundation of the Word of God in my life.

I want to thank my spiritual children, Pastors Tony and Trineene Hall, who are the epitome of commitment and devotion.

All my love to my amazing Mother, Mrs. Emma Ricks. The energy she exudes emanates from her and galvanizes me and everyone she meets.

Lastly, but most certainly not least, I send nothing but love and gratitude to my Faith in Action Family for their unwavering love and inspiration.

Introduction

There is nothing more powerful than the Active Living Word of God. Since receiving the Revelation of just how powerful the Word is, my life has never been the same. My entire existence was revolutionized the moment I began to not only read the Word but embody it.

The key lies in decreeing the Word of God. As it is written in Job 22:28 (King James Version), "Thou shalt also decree a thing, and it shall be established unto thee: and the light shall shine upon thy ways." This verse shows how potent the Word of God is when it is spoken with faith and utter conviction.

According to Romans 10:17, "faith comes by hearing." You undoubtedly know how potent words, or even songs, can be when they are heard repeatedly. They begin to live in your heart. Your role as a believer is to become so unshakably convinced of the veracity and realness of everything written, that it stands as a fortress in your heart, unwavering and without reproach.

The Psalmist expressed that he kept the Word hidden in his heart so he wouldn't sin against Thee (Psalm 119:11). Think of how dynamic this verse is! It places no boundary between God and His Word! When you ingest the Word, you are becoming one with the very Author of that Word, which is God Almighty!

In this book, I will reveal the secrets that I have learned as it pertains to accessing the *Power of God* that has been unleashed to those who truly believe. I pray that as the Powers become realized in your consciousness, the Mind of Christ will be restored to its rightful position on the throne of your life so you can step into your true position and possess everything your Heavenly Father has already left as your inheritance.

CHAPTER ONE

The Power of Study

A lways seek to be an eternal student. Learning should not end simply because you are no longer in a primary school or some other structured educational environment. If you genuinely want to tap into the greatness that has been deemed your birthright, you must have understanding. Proverbs 4:7 boldly states, "that even when gaining wisdom, it is vital for you to get an understanding." To really understand something, you MUST study it.

The Believer Perpetually Retains the Curiosity and Wonder of a Student

Becoming a student of the Word of God takes you on a never-ending journey that is full of deeper insights at every turn. You begin to retain and assimilate the written Word in such a way that it's nearly impossible for it to be taken away from you. Proverbs 4:23 instructs the hearer to keep their heart with all diligence for out of it flows the issues of life.

The word "keep" in Hebrew is the word Shamar. The root of this word means "to guard." When used in a positive manner, guarding protects and maintains. Conversely, if the guards of a city are compromised, the place can easily be besieged by opposing forces. What are you allowing in your heart, Let's utilize the Power of Study to get it out.

Maintaining The Guard Through the *Power of Study*

It's not possible to guard something that is not there. So, the first step to accessing the Penetrating Power of The Word of God is to harness the *Power of Study*. You must know the Word so you can guard it accordingly. Keeping, or, guarding, refers to maintaining the things entrusted to you, particularly the truths of God in faith, action and mind.

The Word is the Final Will & Testament of God. Imagine if a loved one left you a considerable amount of money in their earthly Will but you did not know or couldn't quite comprehend what was written in the document.

This leaves your assets open to being snatched by a trustee or other beneficiary who *did* take the initiative to read through the information and grab it from beneath you! The entire time you were walking around as a very rich individual but because you had no knowledge of the truths listed in the Will passed on to you by your wealthy relative, you unwittingly lived no better than a pauper or someone residing just above the poverty line.

The *Power of Study* Removes Mental Darkness

This is what happens when you don't devote yourself to the *Power of Study*. The enemy can rip your inheritance away because you just don't know what you truly have access to.

Studying the Word of God opens your eyes to not only understanding how much has been entrusted to you, but also gives you the keys to accessing it. This knowledge according to (I Peter 2:9), calls you out of darkness and places you into His marvelous Light, the place of Illumination and Revelation.

David, the Psalmist, spoke so poignantly about the importance of keeping and guarding the Word of God. He speaks about keeping the precepts even when facing the lies of others in Psalm 119:69, which reads;

> "The proud have forged a lie against me: but I will
> keep thy precepts with my whole heart."

Psalm 34:13 also talks about keeping the tongue from evil, showing how the Word you have hidden in your heart is able to bridle your mouth regardless of what outer circumstances appear.

Your Inner Heart Reflects Outwardly

There is no doubt that your life will reflect what is being kept in your heart. You may have heard someone say, "He has issues," as it pertains to someone who has problems, especially of an emotional nature. Another common saying is, "She's so guarded." This refers to an individual who isn't easy to get to know, usually because of old wounds that remain lodged in the heart.

Many of these issues come about because of accidental circumstances that the person couldn't handle at the time they occurred.

Without the proper brain development, training and psychological tools, it's hard to process events that seem unfair or unjust. The natural tendency is to shut down, but the *Power of Study* can change all of this!

Consider this: You may be reading this book on a computer, and the computer was initially built to mimic the way your very own brain works. A computer consists of a central processing unit (CPU) that processes the information that enters it. Although you're able to hop on the Internet very easily with a capable device, going online is actually an extremely intricate process. If you could see the data as it is streamed from the Internet through your processor it would probably look like gibberish to you. The CPU receives the input and processes it, so your eyes see words and images. This is the normal way a computer functions when it is healthy and there is nothing stopping this flow in the background.

However, if you've ever had a virus on your computer, you probably remember how your unit could no longer process the information because the processor was corrupted. Sentences appeared jumbled and the pictures were no longer viewable because of the infection.

The *Power of Study* Renews Your Mind

Studying the Word of God renews your processor (brain) so it can interpret incoming information according to knowledge and truth.

When you begin to study the Word, you no longer process according to the information you've been given by the world's system since the day you arrived on the planet.

James 1:21 instructs the reader to receive with meekness the engrafted Word, which is able to save your souls. So many people have wounded souls because they were overwhelmed with circumstances during a time when they were processing with corrupted files. A particularly traumatic event can shock the brain and nervous system so much that the individual who was subjected to the wound begins to see the world through an entirely different lens! Understand that before being saved by the Grace of the Lord and the Blood of Christ Jesus, nearly every person on the planet walked around with some level of mental bondage. That is the nature of living in a Fallen State.

Studying the Word begins to change your processor back to the original design, which actually never went away but just needs to be reactivated and regerminated with the penetrating Word of God!

There Is Much to Learn By Studying Seed Growth

Germination is the word that describes what happens as seeds develop into new plants. First, environmental conditions must trigger the seed to grow. You may start to feel the calling and unction of God as He extends the invitation for you to accept Him into your heart. You listened to the promptings and contritely confessed unto salvation.

Feelings of hopefulness began to sprout up, causing you to want to find out more about your Savior and the new purpose you are being led to fulfill. This gives you the perfect breeding ground to begin to study the Word with enthusiasm and vigor.

Next, when water is plentiful, the seed fills with the liquid in a process called imbibition, which is a term that describes what happens as one substance is absorbed by another. Consistent studying is the equivalent of the watering process because you begin to become more and more aligned with who you really are, and the old way of thinking and behaving is swallowed up into the newness of life. The water then activates special proteins called enzymes and this begins the process of seed growth.

Because the natural realm closely mimics the Spiritual one, the above illustration demonstrates what the Word of God is capable of doing once it is planted in our hearts. There are many mental as well as physical things to overcome that can only in some cases happen by absorbing the Word. The *Power of Study* opens you up to the germination process because it arms you with the truth.

You'll be able to shed those old, limiting beliefs and concepts that were picked up through folklore, fables and sometimes even family, so you can receive the word and walk in your true heritage.

Let The Word Be Your Guard

As you continue in the *Power of Study*, you'll begin to see that the Word you are guarding *becomes* a guard. The Word starts, "casting down imaginations, and every high thing that exalts itself against the knowledge of God and brings into captivity every thought to the obedience of Christ" (II Corinthians 10:5). The Word is a ruthless guard that throws anything unlike itself into the fiery jails of hell! You'll learn that "the weapons of your warfare are not carnal but mighty through God through the pulling down of strongholds" (II Corinthians 10:4), so you don't have to resort to merely human tactics to fight a spiritual battle. God's mighty weapons are available to us as we fire back against Satan's strongholds. All of this becomes clear as day when you employ the *Power of Study*.

Become Militant About the *Power of Study*

I am adamant about the *Power of Study* because it applies to so many different facets of life. As a veteran of the US Army, I had to devote countless hours of time to study when I became a drill sergeant. From my learning and knowledge of warfare,

I understand that some battle plans can only be handled by a General or a Colonel. It was vital for me to fully comprehend my line of authority because overstepping it could have severe consequences. Choosing to remain ignorant of rank would not be an excuse if a violation occurred, so it was absolutely vital for me to study so I could retain my position. This was the training ground that taught me that the *Power of Study* is a military weapon.

Many believers agree that the language of Ephesians 6:12 is military in nature. The passage reads as follows;

> "For we wrestle not against flesh and blood, but against principalities, against powers, against the rulers of the darkness of this world, against spiritual wickedness in high places."

Paul received a revelation of how Satan's kingdom was aligned militarily. At the top of Satan's dark domain, there is a group of demons called principalities. Principality derives from the word 'arche,' an old term that is used symbolically to denote the leader or being at the very top of the hierarchy. It is also used to denote individuals who hold the loftiest positions of rank and authority.

Powers are the next group mentioned in the text which is followed by **Rulers** of darkness. Powers and Rulers can be both incarnate, such as people who hold high-ranking positions in the world, and they can also be discarnate beings that perform wickedness in nefarious ways. As I stated above, you can see how the natural and spiritual dimensions are reflections of each other just by comparing the filings to visible ranks in each branch of the military.

Understand Who the Real Enemy Is

You must **know your enemy** in order to defeat him. At some point in your Christian life, you'll undoubtedly come into direct contact with evil forces from one of the groups I just listed. Ordinarily, you would naturally assume that your boss has it out for you, your spouse is trying to get under your skin, or your children have reached an age where they want to rebel and stop listening to you. All of these are common occurrences so it might not be apparent that you could be under a spiritual attack. It is at this moment when the *Power of Study* will come into play. You can then go up against the REAL forces that are seeking to undermine you because, "for the weapons of our warfare are not carnal, but mighty through God to the pulling down of strong holds" (II Corinthians 10:4).

As you persist in the *Power of Study,* you'll be able to "cast down imaginations and every high thing that exalts itself against the knowledge of God," that you have disgested (II Corinthians 10:5). No more ruminating over past hurts or feeling slighted at every turn. You have the power to push away the very same thoughts that once plagued you. This ability alone is worth every second you spend pouring over the scriptures.

The *Power of Personalizing* the Word of God

When you study the Word, personalize it. Each verse in the Bible contains gems that are meant to be the normal way of living for every Believer.

For example, when I am meditating on Ephesians 1:17, I say out loud, "That the God of our Lord Jesus Christ, the Father of Glory, may give unto me, Marvin Smith, the spirit of wisdom and revelation in the knowledge of Him." This is a very potent scripture because while you are utilizing the *Power of Study* you want the "Words of God to become flesh," and this can only happen through the quickening Power of the Almighty God.

Make Your Studies A Discipline

Continuing in the *Power of Study* will require discipline, organization and commitment. All these terms come to mind when you think about soldiers.

Regardless of the weather they must train and prepare because sooner or later they will face an enemy that is determined to defeat them. Also, although they are now widely called "majors," there used to be a time when a college advisor or counselor would ask you what "discipline" you wanted to study. They knew it was going to take an enormous amount of discipline to make it through a rigorous course of study and come out victorious on the other end as a university graduate.

This is how you must look at the *Power of Study*. Select a time slot that you can use to study the Word each and every day. A good starting point to kick off your new practice is the Biblical book of John. Read through each chapter in John and then go back to the beginning with Genesis to read about the Origin of Creation. If you want to gain an even deeper understanding, I advise you to get a concordance. Strong's Concordance is an excellent version because you can look up any words you are unfamiliar with and gain even more insight. Just know that this is the beginning of a journey that is sure to reward you in ways you never thought possible.

NOTES

CHAPTER TWO

The Power of Imagination

T he *Power of Imagination* is totally amazing. As with anything, the imagination can be a force for good or a force for evil. Automatically, your imagination seems to run on its own, often in channels you would rather not venture into.

However, the truth is that when you harness the *Power of Imagination* you can accomplish feats that would seem impossible by worldly standards.

Natural and Spiritual Laws Mirror Each Other

Much of this center around the laws. There are natural laws and spiritual laws. What's true in the spiritual realm is also true in the natural.

Natural law is a system of rules that a particular country or community recognizes as regulating the actions of its citizens and which it may enforce by imposing stiff penalties, such as going to court or being imprisoned.

Natural law also pertains to scientific laws that would appear to be unbreakable. One of these is the "Law of Gravity." You've probably heard the saying, "What goes up, must come down." This is a phrase that describes the force of gravity because it causes everything that goes up to fall back down to Earth. Many assume this law is unbendable, but what about airplanes?

There are two forces that work directly against the possibility of flight: Drag and gravity. The wings on a plane must be designed to not only produce lift, but to also minimize friction with passing air. This phenomenon is known as drag. Then, every plane has a specific takeoff speed where lift overcomes gravity. A tilted wing allows more lift to be created at a lower speed.

A propeller or jet engine is installed within the plane so that air is pulled in and simultaneously pushed out in the opposite direction, creating thrust. Thrust and lift are artificially created forces used to supersede nature and enable an airplane to take flight. As a result, the wings overcome the force of gravity and the plane can soar to heights that defy the laws of science.

I wrote that lengthy explanation of just what it takes for an airplane to move through the air because I want to paint a vivid picture of how many components come into play for even the shortest flight.

What kind of mind would even think to bypass what appears to be the irrefutable Law of Gravity, and choose instead to dream bigger?

Orville and Wilbur Wright, also known as the Wright Brothers, are credited with inventing, building and flying the first motor-powered aircraft. Their ability to dream provided the impetus for them to create, recreate, start over, and finally design an airplane. Without their perseverance, the people of the world today may have limited access to other continents because the airplane makes intercontinental travel much faster, allowing passengers to arrive on foreign soil within a timeframe that would not be possible using ships or other methods. I don't know if the Wright Brothers were consciously aware of the *Power of Imagination*, but they most definitely operated in and succeeded because of it!

It All Starts in The Mind

Before the airplane could show up in the tangible world it had to be a thought in the minds of the Wright Brothers. As they meditated and pictured the plane more frequently, it began to "flesh" out and take a definite form in their imaginations. The thoughts eventually became words and the words built up their faith, causing them to be fully persuaded that they could indeed build an airplane. Based on my readings about the Wright Brothers, they were so committed to turning the plane into a reality that they never married, never smoked, drank, or gambled. Wilbur is famously quoted as saying, "I don't have time for both a wife and an airplane." This is the kind of extreme dedication that is needed when you want to put the *Power of Imagination* to work in your own life.

Hebrews 11:1 gives us the ultimate definition of faith. It's described as, "the substance of things hoped for, the evidence of things unseen." The Wright Brothers carved out an invisible image of an airplane and spoke about it so much that they were moved to action. This is a vital point because faith without corresponding works is dead (James 2:17).

The *Power of Imagination* Increases Your Faith

What do you desire that appears to defy natural law? Scriptures says, "all things are possible to them that believe" (Mark 9:23). When you begin to prize the written Word of God over even your own physical senses, you are tapping into the *Power of Imagination*. Regardless of what you see or hear, you can turn away from it and rush to the reality of the supernatural rules, "against such there is no law " (Galatians 5:23). Faith is not a vague hope grounded in fantasy or wishful thinking. Faith is a settled confidence that something in the future will happen because God makes it so. Faith is not blind trust in the face of contrary evidence, and it is not an unknowable leap in the dark. Faith is an inflexible, adamant, unwavering trust in the Everlasting God Who is the All Powerful, Infinitely Wise, Eternally Trustworthy POWER, endlessly revealing Himself through His Word and in the Person of Jesus Christ. His promises have proven true from generation to generation.

I get excited just thinking about it! Hallelujah! All praises to the Most High God! "Unto Him be Glory in the Church by Christ Jesus, throughout all ages, world without end " (Ephesians 3:21) Selah!

Faith causes doors to both open and close. Faith forbids demons and demands action. Faith refuses to allow a promise to be stolen. Faith is not demonstrated by a person who believes in the words, "maybe, possibly, somehow, or someday." No, THAT IS NOT FAITH! Faith is a directed energy that focuses on the target. It is a knowing that is fully persuaded and cannot be deterred. You are already diligently seeking through the *Power of Study* and your seeking will surely be rewarded (Hebrews 11:6). The Lord does not see as man sees; he sees the contents of your heart. I Samuel 16:7 reads as follows:

> "But the Lord said unto Samuel, look not on his countenance, or on the height of his stature; because I have refused him: for the Lord seeth not as man seeth; for man looketh on the outward appearance, but the Lord looketh on the heart."

The faith you have hidden in your heart is like a lighthouse, sending out a clear light that is visible to the Most High. The light becomes brighter and brighter with each passing day.

Once it reaches a critical level, it can no longer be ignored!

Activate The *Power Of Imagination* By Knowing Who You Are

You were made in the image of God (Genesis 1:26 – 28). God calls forth that which is unseen into reality. The word image can also be translated as "In our imagination." In the Hebrew text the term "image" is 'TSELEM,' which means a shadow of, resemblance or representation. This RESEMBLANCE is our spiritual makeup, or DNA. Man was made in the imagination of God before he became a physical REPRESENTATION in the Earth. We were also created with an imagination, one that worked perfectly until the Fall of Man. When The Fall happened, man fell into vain imaginations as opposed to the fully functioning, divine imagination that he was born with.

Christ came to restore the spiritual imagination, causing you to be renewed in the spirit of your mind and giving you back the *Superpower of Imagination* to create the life you deserve.

Now, I understand that everyone has different desires but many of the things you want likely center around perfect health, prosperity, the salvation of your loved ones, and peace. These are universal longings that affect nearly everyone during one period or another. Right now, these cravings might seem like they can never be fulfilled. That's what your senses are telling you. But what does the Word say? You have the right to use the *Power of Imagination* to call your blessings from the Heavenly Realm into this one.

Your imagination can become a portal, bridging the gap between heaven and earth so you're able to make your desires and promises to show up in due season.

The Powers Work in Conjunction With Each Other

This is where you'll bring in what you've learned using the *Power of Study* and combine it with the *Power of Imagination*. When you study, look for verses that specifically apply to the good you want to manifest in your own life. Create a picture in your mind of exactly what you desire. Once you have a clear, concise image imprinted in the neural pathways of your brain, tap into what it would feel like to have it.

Next, speak aloud the scripture that outlines the promise. These are three clear, concise activities that operate like a three-fold chord on a piano. The chord delivers one of the strongest vibrations when it contains at least a three-part harmony. This is truly a dynamic triad that can be so robust that you are overtaken by your heart's desire before you ever thought it could happen!

NOTES

CHAPTER THREE

The Power of Ability

H ebrews 4:12 says, "For the Word of God is quick and powerful, and sharper than any two-edged sword, piercing even to the dividing asunder of soul and spirit, and of the joints and marrow, and is a discerner of the thoughts and intents of the heart."

The Word of God Can Reach Places Inaccessible to
Non-Believers

The Word of God is living and active, having the ability to reach places unhindered where nothing else can go.

Not only that, but its penetrating power is greater than any double-edged sword and reaches the innermost being, of a person so that it judges the thoughts and attitudes of the heart.

In doing this, it can discriminate successfully between what is spiritual in man and what is merely "soulish," or, natural.

Understand that the Word of God penetrates even to the dividing of soul and spirit and does so even when these often-contradictory inner elements are interwoven as closely as joints and marrow.

The Word can cut through damaged emotions and push low self-worth into the Sea of Forgetfulness. It destroys traumatic experiences and psychological discord, repairing the residual damage never to be seen again.

I want you to have a rock-solid expectation in the ability of the Word of God. The *Power of Ability* is all about you KNOWING that the Word of The Almighty is sure. The *Power of Study* and the *Power of Imagination* are designed to get you to the point of fully possessing the *Power of Ability.*

Through your studies and creative imagination, you'll eventually arrive at a place where you have absolutely no doubt in the *Power of the Ability* that resides in the Word. Much of what I've learned has come through extensive experience, but if you are willing to vigilantly follow the precepts in this book, you can move leaps ahead and avoid some of the hard knocks that can come as a result of ignorance.

Strive For Astuteness in The Things of God

When I first began, I was not astute in spirituality. The word 'astute' means having an ability to accurately assess situations or people and turn this to one's advantage. Let me tell you a story that demonstrates what happens when you ARE NOT astute.

A mother and father came to me about their adopted daughter, who was apparently demon-possessed. Their daughter had a Doctoral level degree and at one time was working in a position where she made a substantial amount of money. Because I was not astute, I equated her expansive education with her having a skill set she actually did not have. I assumed that since she had obtained her learning through teaching, I would only have to give her verbal instructions to see change. I simply advised her to replace negative thoughts with positive ones and try to recall good memories such as spending time with family during the holidays.

Little did I know, this was not the answer. She looked at me and her eyes doubled in size and turned red. Strange sounds started coming out of her mouth and she turned to try to run out of the church. It took both me and her father to catch her. The father took her to their vehicle, and I went back to speak with her mother.

The mother explained to me that the changes in her daughter began when she found out she was adopted. After the young woman's aunt told her who her real father was, she went on a search and found him in another state. Keep in mind, she did not call her biological father or alert him in any way prior to making her way to his home and ringing the doorbell. It just so happened that her father opened the door and inquired about who she was. She stated, "I'm your daughter. My mother told me about you." He looked at his daughter and said, "Don't you ever come to this house again," and slammed the door in her face.

Her biological mother had rejected her at birth by giving her up for adoption and now she had to deal with a second round of rejection from her father all over again. The compounded rejection from her father proved to be too much for her psyche to handle and that sent her on a downward spiral.

Constant barrages of thoughts led to demonic oppression that completely changed the way she behaved and responded. I advised the parents to seek professional psychological assistance for her.

Before that experience, she was singing in the choir and was very active in her church. All of that came to a screeching halt and the last thing I heard about her was that she was in a mental institution.

Becoming Astute Builds Confidence in The *Power of Ability*

I relayed this story because there is a connection between ability and astuteness. From that experience, I learned that a rock-solid faith in ability comes from being astute. After giving myself over to the *Power of Study,* the Lord has used me to cast demons out of multiple people. The joy that comes over me when I see someone set free from demonic torment is so vast that I can hardly put it into words.

The *Power of Ability* comes to the forefront when you study to show yourself approved (II Timothy 2:15). This endows you with the blessed assurance that you will be instructed in any and every situation by the Holy Spirit so you will know what moves to make. Heeding the guidance reinforces your belief in the Ability of God to keep you and in your own ability to hear and receive the constant messages that are given to you by the Lord. When something happens in your life such as a bad report from a doctor or someone in your family runs into trouble, you know you can go to The Rock which is higher than yourself for answers and reassurance. Your faith in this ability transitions your thinking from a place of worry, fear or anxiety into one that is full of perfect peace.

Transitioning refers to the process of changing from one state or condition to another. This may not be easy to do at first, but constantly utilizing the Powers builds up the muscle of ability until you find yourself readily able to fend off the fiery darts of the adversary.

Build Faith in The *Power of Ability* with Repetition

We now know that "faith comes by hearing and hearing by the Word of God " (Romans 10:17). We also know that we are to meditate on the word both day and night. Practicing the Powers lodges the Word into your spirit so when the harmful thoughts come at a rapid pace you have a fortified inner man there to sustain you.

The composition of Man consists of spirit, soul and body. The real you are a spirit, you have a soul which refers to your mind, will and emotions, and you live in a human body. Our bodies are vessels that contain our spirit and are made of dust that will return to the dust.

Without a spirit, a human body is little more than a meat suit. The spirit that animates the body makes it an honorable vessel that was made by the very Hand of God. This magnificent body is a vessel that contains our assignment helpers that promote the Glory of God and allow us to fulfill our purpose on the Earth. The darts can hit any one of these facets of your being but when you are armed with the *Power of Ability*, you'll know what to do to handle the assault.

Understanding The Inner Composition of Man

Because gaining an intense understanding of the concepts you hear is so important, I'm going to go a bit further into your overall makeup. I like to look at the body as the Outer Court, the soul as the Inner Court and the Spirit as the Holy of Holies. The Word of God must get into the Holy of Holies facet of your being for you to truly realize it's effectiveness. Along with hearing the Word and meditating on it, you can also pierce the Holy Place with the Word through soaking. Soaking or marinating is incredibly powerful and if you've ever marinated a piece of meat, you can better understand the difference it makes in tenderness and taste.

Marinating and soaking is all based on time. Most people marinate meat overnight so the herbs and spices can all come together and fully penetrate the meat. In much the same way, you must spend time soaking in the Word, so it gets into your spirit and transforms your mind. The *Power of Ability* that comes through the soaking process casts away fear so you can operate in the sound mind spoken about in II Timothy 1:7 with all confidence.

Have you ever been under so much pressure that you couldn't think straight and almost felt like you were losing it? This is a common human experience when you dwell in the Fallen State. Marinating increases the *Power of Ability* within you so when the pressures of life come your way you can tackle them from the sound mind, which is your natural state of being.

Your Real Mental and Emotional Existence

Let me give you a glimpse of what it will be like when you view the world from a sound mind.

The term "sound mind" is taken from the Greek word "sophroneo", which is a compound word combining sodzo and phrneo. It suggests something that is delivered, rescued, revived, salvaged, and protected, now resting in a safe place that is completely secure. Having this kind of mind girds you up when you would ordinarily be tempted to succumb to fear, giving you a fierce outlook that makes you invincible in the face of dangers seen and unseen. Your logic is fully intact, and the rationality of this logic guides your emotions, so they stay on an even keel.

As you can see, this is a totally different kind of mind than what the average person dwells in on a regular basis. However, when the Word gets into your spirit and causes the Divine Reversal that switches you back into your Original state, your sound mind becomes the driver of your life, changing the way you focus and restoring your emotional balance.

Why is it important for you to know all of this?

Because it contributes to you attaining the *Power of Ability* in very major ways. When you know that God wants you to be able to stand no matter what is happening around you and has equipped you with the mind to be able to do it, this increases your faith even more and takes you one step closer to grasping ahold to the Promises.

NOTES

CHAPTER FOUR

The Power of Avoidance

N ow, more than ever before, it is absolutely VITAL for you to exercise the *Power of Avoidance*. So much of the contamination that people are experiencing in these times is a direct result of social media consumption. I have never in my life seen so many virtual prophets and pastors with huge followings where the people DO NOT KNOW THEM.

The Bible clearly says in I Thessalonians 5:12;

> "And we beseech you, brethren, to know them which
> labor among you, and are over you in the Lord, and
> admonish you."

Now, please don't misunderstand my statement, there are indeed men and women of God that I personally listen too that I was introduced to via an online platform. However, they have proven to have tested and fruitful ministries and I'm careful to investigate their lives before ingesting their words. On the other hand, I also know of men and women on social media who profess to be of the fold, but don't even LIKE people. They are truly only operating their ministries to see what their followers can do for them. These wolves in sheep's clothing are contaminating the minds of the masses with belief systems that are totally contrary to the Word of God. Constantly listening to the venom, they put out over the airwaves can be very detrimental to your life.

There Are Both Good and Evil Shepherds

II John 1:10-11 says;

> "If there come any unto you, and bring not this doctrine, receive him not into your house neither bid him God speed. For he that biddeth him God speed is partaker of his evil deeds."

There are people in the social media world who are on an assignment that has nothing to do with God but is of Satan. They may not even realize this is the case because they could be so blinded by their own deficiencies. These individuals pollute the Word of God with false doctrines that are most likely born out of unhealed pain and spew it out to kindred spirits.

You see, most people will only truly hear a message that resonates with them. Therefore, you have entire platforms built around coddling psychological issues because the people involved can relate to the messenger. In these cases, the rooms they gather in become echo chambers where every person is essentially saying and believing the same thing, not even understanding that they need deliverance and not a co-signer!

If you or someone you know is following speakers like these then the Bible says you are a partaker of their evil deeds. In the Amplified version of the Bible, II Corinthians 11:13-15 states;

> "For such men are false apostles (spurious, counterfeits,) deceitful workmen, masquerading as apostles (special messengers) of Christ. (14) And no wonder, for Satan himself masquerades as an angel of light. (15) So, it is no great surprise if his servants also masquerade as servants of righteousness, but their end will correspond with their deeds."

The aforementioned scriptures detail just how easy it is for someone to impersonate one of God's elect and lead so many people astray.

Satan is incredibly subtle. We are warned that he uses professing men of God (ministers of righteousness) to deceive the Church. The Bible calls Satan the God of this world.

He loves nothing more than to use the *power of the airwaves* that bring you all forms of telecommunications (television, radio, cellular devices, and the internet), to interrupt your destiny and steer you down a path of destruction. Technology has evolved to such an extent that it requires little more than a mobile phone with camera capabilities to start a virtual ministry and gain traction. There is no longer anyone there to test a person who wants to begin a ministry and without checks and balances, there is bound to be trouble.

The Importance of Being Commissioned and Appointed

I Timothy 1:14 reads;

> "Neglect not the gift that is in thee, which was given to you by prophecy, with the laying on of hands of the presbytery."

Let's break down the word 'presbytery'. The presbytery is ordinarily made up of leaders representing the five-fold ministry, such as apostles, bishops, pastors, and elders. Their role is the oversight and administration of the church. This verse outlines that the presbytery oftentimes is spiritually aware of the next person who is being called into a higher role because they are prompted by the Spirit of God.

In the Bible, we see this with Timothy because he received a gift through the Apostle Paul through the laying on of hands, something that is commonly associated with the continuity of leadership. This phenomenon is written in both Testaments, with one distinct passage from the Old Testament being detailed in Deuteronomy 34:9:

"And Joshua the son of Nun was full of the Spirit of Wisdom; For Moses had laid his hands upon him: and the Children of Israel hearkened unto him and did as the Lord commanded Moses."

This indicates that Joshua was to be the successor to Moses and God demonstrated this by giving him a supernatural ability to lead, which was so necessary for someone in charge of such a huge flock. Moses had walked with Joshua for many years and deeply knew his spirit. This allowed him to "pass the torch" with all confidence because the mantle would be in good hands.

How God sent Leaders Protect Their Flocks

A true leader always seeks to make his or her followers less susceptible to satanic contamination. The leader does this by teaching the *Power of Avoidance*. Keep in mind that the avoidance I am referring to is an ACTIVE AVOIDANCE. Avoidance refers to, "The action of keeping away from or not doing something." It is a definite ACT that must be put into practice. When you come up against a situation, person or event that is in direct opposition to the Word you have hidden in your heart, you immediately turn away from such a thing before it even has a chance to take root.

I would be remiss if I didn't advise you, the reader, to sincerely ask the Lord to bestow upon you the spirit of discernment. This one quality alone can help you avoid the contamination that lies in wait for both innocent and experienced souls alike, who aren't aware of the pitfalls that await them in the virtual world.

The New Testament also places an emphasis on the transference of a righteous calling. Acts 6:1-7 states;

> "And in those days, when the number of the disciples was multiplied there arose a murmuring of the Grecians against the Hebrews, because their widows were neglected in the daily ministration. Then the twelve called the multitude of the disciples unto them, and said, "It is no reason that we should leave the Word of God and serve tables. Wherefore brethren, look ye out among you seven men of honest report, full of the Holy Ghost and wisdom whom we may appoint over this business. But we will give ourselves continually to prayer, and to the ministry of the Word. And the saying pleased the whole multitude: and they chose Stephen, a man full of faith and of the Holy Ghost, and Philip, and Prochorus, and Nicanor, and Timon, and Parmenas, and Nicolas a proselyte of Antioch: Whom they set before the apostles: and when they had prayed, they laid their hands on them. And the **Word of God** increased; and the number of disciples multiplied in Jerusalem greatly; and a great company of the priests were obedient to the faith."

Again, these passage refers to how the Biblical selection process works. The Elders found men with upright spirits who could handle many of the day-to-day tasks, such as caring for the needs of the widows, so that those in higher positions could devote themselves completely to prayer and total consecration. They evaluated the character of each candidate and went to the Lord in prayer to receive guidance as they made their choices.

Once they had the "green light," they conferred the Anointing for Service through the laying on of hands.

Avoidance is NOT an Option

Moving in the *Power of Avoidance* is not an option in this hour. You must be extremely careful of who you give a listening ear to. This ties in with the *Power of Study* because when the Word is deeply embedded in your heart, you should feel a nudging when listening to a person who has not been deemed worthy by tried-and-true men and women of God, and sanctioned by The Creator. That individual could be operating out of a spirit of rebellion because they didn't want to undergo the years of training that it sometimes takes to develop the Fruit of the Spirit and the unction that can only be endowed from above.

The satanic contamination that can come out of these situations could set you back for a very long time. Knowing the difference between charisma and true Anointing can keep you from being sucked in by a set of beguiling words that may sound pleasant to the ears but, in the end, head downward toward Hell.

Once you learn that a particular person is not operating in the right Spirit, you must cut them off immediately. According to the Scriptures, failing to do so makes you an accessory to their misdeeds. If you're following such a one or are subscribed to their channel, take extreme measures right away. Unsubscribe from anyone that isn't adhering to the tenets of our Faith and unfollow those same individuals across all social platforms.

Try to get better insight into the true status of their lives. Anyone can paint a sparkling picture when all you can see is what they are presenting online. Be watchful and prayerful and use the *Power of Avoidance* because it is there for the believer as a mighty form of protection to keep you on The Path.

NOTES

CHAPTER FIVE

The Power of Attending

T he *Power of Attending* is a culminating force that brings all of the other Powers together and places them under a magnifying glass. The fourth chapter of the book of I Timothy so poignantly lays out what it will require for you to stand in the fullness of the promises of God.

Verses 1–2 and 6–13 of the fourth chapter of I Timothy, speak about what will happen during the last days. These scriptures are dynamic and authoritative because the Apostle Paul explains exactly what you should avoid as well as do during the end times to receive the inheritance. You must ATTEND to the Powers so you can walk in them. It will require extreme discipline because as the previous scriptures say, you will need to block out all the external noise that doesn't adhere to the doctrine of the Word of God.

Those negative reports from friends and Family – block them out. The ways of the world that are followed by the masses but do not line up with the Scriptures? Active avoidance is necessary.

Your job as a believer is to Attend (I Timothy 4:13) to the Powers of Study, Imagination, Ability and Avoidance to such an extent that you can't literally SEE NOR HEAR ANYTHING ELSE.

As it is written in Deuteronomy 30:19;

> "I call heaven and earth to record this day against
> you, that I have set before you life and death, blessing
> and cursing: therefore, choose life, that both thou
> and thy seed may live:"

This is how strong your belief must be. When you reach that pinnacle moment where your faith in the outside world tips the scales and switches to become an unwavering knowing in the world inside of you, this is when you spiritually sign on the dotted line and claim the birthright that was always there for the taking.

If you've ever gone to a wedding or some other gathering, you were said to be in ATTENDANCE. This means you were present and could be counted by your visibility. People who never showed up may hear about the occasion via word-of-mouth, but there is only so much they can know if they weren't actually there. Only the guests in physical attendance were privy to everything that took place. Therefore, their experience of the festivities will be much more vivid than if they had second-hand information.

This is how you want to view the notion of ATTENDING to the Word of God. Yes, you should definitely be part of a Bible-believing church where the pastor is teaching and preaching the inspired Word of God.

However, until you begin to activate the Powers by doing your own studying, meditating, imagining, and avoiding, all the words remain as passive rhetoric that don't really have true bearing in your life.

Walking In the Power of Attending

Making ATTENDANCE part of your everyday journey ignites a fire and passion that you just can't get from outside observation.

The sixteenth chapter of the book of Matthew lists several scriptures regarding how the believer has been given several Keys. The verses illustrate that there are multiple keys to the Kingdom of Heaven. It's a majestic Kingdom, ever eternal on High.

This means that we have already been given all the abundance we could hope for, but we need the right Key to unlock the door to the spiritual room we wish to enter.

There is a Heavenly Key that will unlock the door to any domain of life that we desire. Some of these include the Keys of Healing, Deliverance, Peace, Joy, and so many more. You can grasp these keys by Attending to the Word of God. Jesus wants us to experience the KEYS OF LIFE, and not just the keys to life. As you remain in the Powers this is sure to become a reality for you.

Learn The *Power of Embracing* the Keys

Jesus loved the Book of Deuteronomy and taught out of it on many occasions.

Deuteronomy is rich in Scripture pertaining to the Keys. In Deuteronomy 4:5-6, it states;

> "Behold, I have taught you statutes and judgments, even as the Lord my God commanded me, that ye should do so in the land wither ye go to possess it. Keep therefore and do them; for this is your wisdom and your understanding in the sight of the nations, which shall hear all these statues, and say, Surely this is a wise people."

These verses focus on wise and understanding people. These are those who comprehend the Keys of the Kingdom. In my experience, understanding is just as important as wisdom.

It's possible to possess great wisdom but have no ability to understand or comprehend it.

Proverbs 4:7 admonishes the reader to always get understanding, even while seeking wisdom.

Wisdom is the principal thing because it is the *power of right judgment* and the ability to choose the correct solution for any situation.

It is knowing how to think, speak, and act to please both God and man throughout life.

Wisdom is the basis for victorious living. Without Wisdom, men make choices that bring pain, poverty, trouble, and even death.

When you have the Key of Wisdom, you make choices that bring health, peace, prosperity, success, and life. Your future depends on your degree of wisdom and understanding.

Understanding helps wisdom fulfill its assignment in a person's life. Understanding is the *power of discernment* and the ability to see past what meets the eye to recognize the actual faults or merits of a thing. It is the ability to grasp a matter or situation and assess it correctly. Without understanding, man is easily deceived and led astray. They become perplexed and confused, unable to deal with the issues of life. However, with understanding, a man can see what others miss to avoid the snares and traps of enticing sins.

> Proverbs 4:20-22
>
> "My son, attend to my words; incline thine ear unto my sayings. Let them not depart from thine eyes; keep them in the midst of thine heart. For they are life unto those that find them, and health to all their flesh."

The major key to life's blessings is Attending to God's Word. Another meaning for the word Attending is "to watch attentively, or, to apply oneself." A central problem I see in the people of the Kingdom of God is a lack of results. This has a direct correlation with failing to Attend. It behooves each of us to make Attending to the Word of God a major priority in our lives.

NOTES

CHAPTER SIX

The Power of Decreeing

T he *Power of Decreeing* the Word of God has revolutionized
my life, ministry and the lives of the many people I have been
blessed to teach. When I was very new in my Christian walk, my
Pastor taught extensively from the book of Romans Chapter 4,
which talks about the faith of Abraham.

Romans 4:17 states;

> "As it is written, I have made thee a father of many
> nations, before him whom he believed, even God,
> who quickeneth the dead, and calleth those things
> which be not as though they were."

God calling those things which are not as though they were, is
an example of the Law of Assumption. The Almighty is so sure of
His Word that when He makes a statement it is as good as finished.
We can see this taking place in Genesis 17: 15-19:

"And God said unto Abraham, as for Sarai thy wife, thou shalt not call her name Sarai, but Sarah shall her name be. And I will bless her, and give thee a son also of her: yea, I will bless her, and she shall be a mother of nations; kings of people shall be of her. Then Abraham fell upon his face, and laughed, and said in his heart, Shall a child be born unto him that is an hundred years old? and shall Sarah, that is ninety years old, bear? And Abraham said unto God, O that Ishmael might live before thee! And God said, Sarah thy wife shall bear thee a son indeed; and thou shalt call his name Isaac: and I will establish my covenant with him for an everlasting covenant, and with his seed after him."

Assumption Makes Your Declarations Sure

Abraham already had a measure of faith because as soon as God told him about the new name for his wife, we see him calling Sarah by that name immediately! However, he was still trying to figure out how he and Sarah were going to defy natural law by having a child at what he considered to be a very advanced age.

Through your study and meditation, you have gained a sure footing in the Word that is becoming more real than anything you can perceive in this material world. The Word has been safeguarded in your heart and has no choice but to come out of your lips.

You must put away your former conversation and put on the new man through the *Power of Decreeing* (Ephesians 4:22-25). Your whole way of speaking and perceiving must be changed, it is also important for you to realize this takes volition. The Bible even says it requires violence and must be taken by force (Matthew 11:12).

Conscious Versus Unconscious Decrees

So much of what you perceive to be conscious behavior is an automatic reflex. This includes both actions and speech. Have you ever noticed that children have a way of speaking in a spontaneous manner that is innocent and usually accurate?

They haven't been completely programmed by the dictates and customs of this world yet, so their words are pure and quite humorous.

As an adult, you've spent many years being unconsciously trained by the systems that govern the social structure of the environment you were born into. This is a good thing to a certain extent because if you act in a manner that is totally opposed to the social graces of your surrounding area you could be perceived as a threat.

The conditioning you've received since birth includes overt, necessary mannerisms such as greeting people with a wave, saying thank you after receiving something, stopping at red lights before proceeding, picking up behind yourself, and all those common customs that make human society possible. However, you've also been implanted with detrimental programs that lead you to believe that you are a mere product of your environment and cannot change. These customs are generally covert because they aren't necessarily taught to you, but they are picked up by observation and mimicry.

The internally programmed customs are the most dangerous because they govern your life without you knowing it. They show up in your automatic thoughts and responses. For example, perhaps you grew up in a poor household and began to believe you could never do better. Or the people around you consumed calorie-dense diets, and all suffered some sort of health affliction when they reached a certain age. You subconsciously digested this material and may think it is your fate as well.

Abandon Automatic Worldly Decrees with the Word of God

This is where the *Power of Decreeing* comes into play. Choose the Scriptures containing promises that are not yet visible in your reality and totally change the way you speak. Forcefully confess that they are now yours and believe wholeheartedly that they will indeed manifest. Use the *Power of Attending* to remain steadfast and watch as the words you decree show up and overtake you with blessings.

Jeremiah, the prophet, tells us that the lord promises to watch "over (His) Word to perform it." Jeremiah could be confident that the spirit of God would accompany the preaching of the prophet, and guarantee that it would accomplish the Lord's intent for it. Jeremiah 1:12, is a counterpart of Mark 16: 20, "And they went forth, and preached everywhere, the Lord working with them, and confirming the word with signs following. Amen. The word confirm means to establish the truth or correctness of (something previously believed, suspected, or feared to be true).

The word decree is a legal term that can mean and authoritative instruction provided by someone who has authority, or by a government. It also means a judgment decided by a court of law.

When we decree God's word, it is alive and full of power to bring itself to pass. According to Isaiah 55:11, it does not return empty but accomplishes everything it is sent out to do. The Power of Decreeing the Word of God is powerful.

The word of God is our strongest weapon for spiritual warfare. Jesus demonstrated this when he rejected satan's temptation in the desert. When he said in the book of Matthew chapter 4:1-11; Jesus told the devil "what was written."

NOTES

CHAPTER SEVEN

The Power of Leadership

II Peter 1:10 reads as follows:

> "Wherefore the rather, brethren, give diligence to make your calling and election sure for if ye do these things, ye shall never fall."

A clarion call is being sent out in this verse. The word 'clarion' is an adjective that means "loud and clear." Peter is asking every Kingdom leader if they are hearing what he's saying. As it relates to the physical church, it is directed toward apostles, prophets, evangelists, pastors, and teachers. However, this scripture is relevant for every believer on this planet.

We each have leadership in some sector of our lives, whether it be on the job or as a parent.

That's why the *Power of Leadership* applies to us all.

Confirm Your Calling

If you serve as a leader in some capacity within the Church, it's your job to edify and teach the members of the Body so they can aspire toward spiritual growth. There really is no way for a newborn Christian who is entering the Church after a lifetime with little to no knowledge about the Word of God to operate in the Powers without a seasoned leader there to guide them on the path. The confirmation of your true calling comes about when you begin to bear fruit.

As a leader, your fruit has a direct correlation to the condition of the people under your tutelage.

Understand the seriousness of what it means to be asked by The Creator of the Universe to lead His people! It is the highest honor that can be bestowed on you and is written about extensively in the Bible.

There are so many components to a true calling, but I want to focus on a few of them below.

The Calling Pre-Dates Birth

> Jeremiah 1:5
> "Before I formed thee in the belly I knew thee; and before thou camest forth out of the womb I sanctified thee, and I ordained thee a prophet unto the nations."

Galatians 1:15

"But when it pleased God, who separated me from my mother's womb, and called me by his grace."

Isaiah 44:2

"Thus saith the Lord that made thee, and formed thee from the womb, which will help thee. Fear not, O Jacob, my servant; and thou, Jesurun, whom I have chosen."

These scriptures are incredibly powerful because they illustrate that the calling occurs even before you open your eyes on the planet.

Ephesians 1:4

"According as he hath chosen us in him before the foundations of the world, that we should be holy and without blame before him in love: " The Lord God Almighty has chosen you, and consecrated you, and set you aside to be part of the Great Commission.

Now, there are some people who seem to know from a very young age that there's a bigger calling on their lives and they walk right into it. However, others tend to live a different kind of life until one day they wake up and realize that they've been selected. I fit into the latter category and am so thankful that God opened my eyes to the truth so I could carry out my purpose with truth and conviction.

The Calling is Initiated by God

John 15:16

"Ye have not chosen me, but I have chosen you, that ye should go and bring forth fruit, and that your fruit should remain: that whatsoever ye shall ask of the Father in my name, he may give it you."

John 6:44

"No man can come to me, except the Father which hath sent me draw him: and I will raise him up at the last day."

II Timothy 1:9

"Who hath saved us, and called us with an holy calling, not according to our works, but according to his own purpose and grace, which was given in Christ Jesus before the world began."

I really want to place a strong emphasis on this aspect of God's calling. In an age where ANYBODY with computer access can literally pay for a ministerial license and instantly set up shop as a teacher or preacher to the public, it is vital for anyone in search of a leader to understand that the calling is INITIATED BY GOD Jeremiah 3:15 reads as follows:

> "And I will give you pastors according to mine heart, which shall feed you with knowledge and understanding."

As I mentioned earlier in the book, established leaders who are known throughout their communities and have an upright spirit and reputation as apostles, bishops, pastors, and elders are usually the people who are anointed by God to ordain those who are to be leaders. Keep in mind that this only happens after these experienced leaders have observed the life of the individual to be ordained and can bear witness to their good fruit, accountability and soundness of mind.

This point **cannot** be driven home hard enough because if you fall into the hands of an individual who was not called by the Lord God Almighty Himself, you could find yourself caught up in a cult-like experience that strips you of the Powers so they can be misused by the misguided and sometimes outright demonic leaders of the organization you linked up with!

The Calling is Costly

I Corinthians 15:31
"I protest by your rejoicing which I have in Christ Jesus our Lord, I die daily."

Luke 9:23
"And he said to them all, if any man will come after me, let him deny himself, and take up his cross daily, and follow me."

Galatians 2:20
"I am crucified with Christ: nevertheless I live; yet not I, but Christ liveth in me: and the life which I now live in the flesh I live by the faith of the Son of God, who loved me, and gave himself for me."

The calling of God does not come without its own share of hardships. You must be prepared to lose friends, family members, opportunities, the favor of the world, and so much more.

A good way to tell if a leader is called is to notice how they respond to the costs associated with the position. Babes in Christ who are operating prematurely in their calling because they haven't learned how to activate The Powers listed in this book, or those who have decided to call themselves, generally won't have the inner strength and fortitude to keep going in the face of adversity.

It takes the tried-and-true testing of the Holy Spirit to withstand the onslaught that can come as you progress in your calling.

This only happens when you truly realize you are dead in Christ and it's no longer you who lives, but Christ who does the Work through you.

Never Stop Learning

There is a mandate across the Earth right now for every man and woman of God to read and study like they never have before. Habakkuk 2:14 reads:

> "For the earth shall be filled with the knowledge of
> the glory of the Lord, as the waters cover the sea."

The kind of information that is literally at your fingertips via your mobile phone was unheard of just a few short years ago.

Anything you want to find out can be accessed in a matter of minutes or seconds so you can apply it on the spot and start seeing the results.

This is an incredible blessing to the people of God. No longer do you have to travel to a Bible bookstore in search of the passages you need to find that contains the information you need. Although this remains as one of my favorite pastimes, I also enjoy the convenience of going online in a flash and using a search engine to pull up out-of-publication books that are almost impossible to locate.

I said all of that to say this: Never stop learning. You should always strive to make your election sure, and this happens when you are committed to continually deepening your well of knowledge so you have even more to pull from to Bless the people of God each time you open your mouth.

Use The *Power of Leadership* to Motivate Others

> Hebrews 10:25
> "Not forsaking the assembling of ourselves together, as the manner of some is; but exhorting one another: and so much the more, as ye see the day approaching."

As leaders, we are commanded to exhort and motivate the people in our local congregation.

This is so critical because the times we live in are especially perilous. It's no longer a secret: These are indeed the last days. You just never know what it can mean to someone who has fallen into a state of depression because of a personal situation to receive a smile and salutation from you as you leave the church building.

It could be the difference between life and death!

Also, as I stated above, leaders come in so many sizes, shapes and forms. If you have children, you are their leader. Let the *Power of Leadership* infuse you with an infectious spirit that makes them so happy to greet the day that they want to make every second count.

The same rules apply in the workplace. If you've been granted a leadership role, do your best to make the job site one that is welcoming, inviting, encouraging, and inspirational. This can only help because a happy staff will generally perform better, increasing productivity, and thereby making the organization more profitable.

NOTES

CONCLUSION

The Holy Librarian

I've found that the spirit moving across the land can be likened to a Holy librarian. The Holy Spirit has been released as a librarian to lead you to the perfect books to read to get to the next level.

Perhaps this is one of the books you were prompted to pick up. If so, you are probably amazed at some of the insights you've gained and are energized about implementing them so you can experience the forward momentum and change you've always desired. I recommend you read the book again, this time highlighting the passages that impressed you and doing some note-taking to point out particularly revelatory pieces.

Get excited about the *Power of the Penetrating* Word and thank God for it Today!

About the Author

Apostle Marvin L. Smith was born and raised in Norfolk, Virginia, and is the son of Emma Ricks as well as the late Charlie Smith. Apostle Marvin Smith is a highly sought-after prophet, preacher and teacher who delivers kingdom mandates to the body of Christ and proclaims the truth of the gospel.

Faith In Action Church began and was founded by Apostle Smith on January 19, 1992. It is a church with a vision and mission of saving lost souls, praising and worshipping God, moving and flowing in the Gifts of the Spirit and meeting the Spiritual needs of the people.

He attended Victory Life Bible College and Norfolk State University. Apostle Smith was affirmed as an Apostle in March of 2004 and has recently released his latest work, "**The Penetrating Power of The Word of God.**"

Apostle Smith is also President of Faith in Action School of Theology, which graduated its first class in 2006. Apostle Smith is a heavily anointed man of God who has a vision to see all come into the knowledge of the love of Christ.

With honor, he was acknowledged and awarded the "Hampton Roads Hero" by FOX 43 NEWS channel for his Outstanding Work in Ministry and the Community in 2012. Apostle Smith is married to Pastor Denise Smith, and they have seven children and eight grandchildren collectively.

NOTES

NOTES

NOTES

NOTES

CPSIA information can be obtained
at www.ICGtesting.com
Printed in the USA
BVHW052015190423
662663BV00009B/132